PIZZA
FOR DINNER

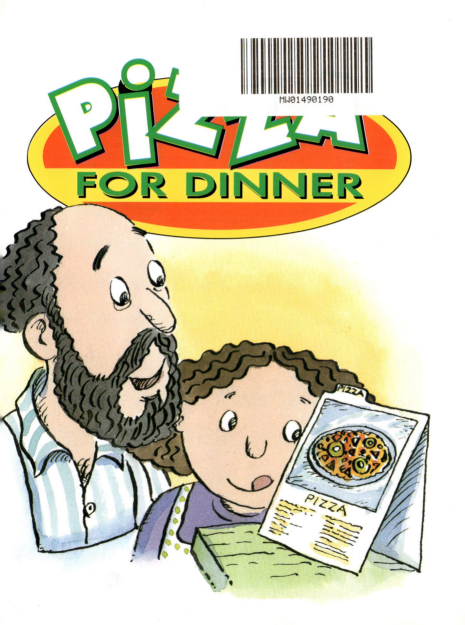

2

"I'm going to make pizza
for dinner," Dad said.

"Yay!" I said.
"Can I make pizza too?"

Dad mixed up the dough
for the pizza.
Then he gave me some.
"Here," he said.
"Roll this for your pizza."
I watched Dad
roll the pizza dough.
Then I copied what he did...

"Now spread some
tomato paste over your pizza,"
said Dad.
I watched Dad spread his pizza.
Then I copied what he did...

8

"Chop up these mushrooms
and put them
on your pizza," said Dad.
I watched Dad
chop up some mushrooms.
Then I copied what he did...

"Let's put some onions
on our pizzas," said Dad.
I watched Dad
put onions on his pizza.
Then I copied what he did...

"Pineapple would be nice,"
said Dad.

"I like pineapple," I said.

"How about cheese?" said Dad.

"Yum!" I said.

"My pizza doesn't look
very beautiful," I said to Dad.

"Don't worry," said Dad.
"It will taste good."

And it did. It tasted great!